RIK EMMETT
REINVENTION
POEMS

ECW

This book is also available as a Global Certified Accessible™ (GCA) ebook. ECW Press's ebooks are screen reader friendly and are built to meet the needs of those who are unable to read standard print due to blindness, low vision, dyslexia, or a physical disability.

Published by ECW Press
665 Gerrard Street East
Toronto, Ontario, Canada M4M 1Y2
416-694-3348 / info@ecwpress.com

MISFIT

Editor for the Press: Michael Holmes / a misFit book

Cover design: Made by Emblem

LIBRARY AND ARCHIVES CANADA CATALOGUING IN PUBLICATION

Title: Reinvention : poems / Rik Emmett.

Names: Emmett, Rik, author.

Identifiers: Canadiana (print) 20210210729 | Canadiana (ebook) 2021021077X

ISBN 978-1-77041-627-7 (softcover)
ISBN 978-1-77305-842-9 (ePub)
ISBN 978-1-77305-843-6 (PDF)
ISBN 978-1-77305-844-3 (Kindle)

Classification: LCC PS8609.M64 R45 2021 | DDC C811/.6—dc23

The publication of *Reinvention* has been generously supported by the Canada Council for the Arts and is funded in part by the Government of Canada. *Nous remercions le Conseil des arts du Canada de son soutien. Ce livre est financé en partie par le gouvernement du Canada.* We acknowledge the support of the Ontario Arts Council (OAC), an agency of the Government of Ontario, which last year funded 1,965 individual artists and 1,152 organizations in 197 communities across Ontario for a total of $51.9 million. We also acknowledge the contribution of the Government of Ontario through the Ontario Book Publishing Tax Credit, and through Ontario Creates for the marketing of this book.

ONTARIO CREATES

ONTARIO ARTS COUNCIL
CONSEIL DES ARTS DE L'ONTARIO
an Ontario government agency
un organisme du gouvernement de l'Ontario

Canada Council for the Arts
Conseil des Arts du Canada
Canada

PRINTED AND BOUND IN CANADA

PRINTING: COACH HOUSE 5 4 3 2 1

To the First Circle — my wife, Jeannette,
always and forever — and my family & friends.

CONTENTS

Preface — Recreational Therapy 1

Part One: The Humanities 3

The Search Is Sacred 4
These Be the Attitudes 6
Self-Confession: Uncommonly Reasonable Secular Agnostic Common Prayer 8
Angels 10
Love Is the Answer 11

Part Two: Life and Death 13

Have a Good Day 14
Dear Diary 16
Game Changer 17
Four Stanzas 19
Ticket to Ride 21
Loss, Grief, Ritual 23
Born to Pay 24
Definitions, Perspective and Choices 26
The Examined Life Is Worth Living 28
Courage of Convictions 29

Part Three: There's Politics in Everything 31

There's Politics in Everything 32
Genders Strangers Foreigners Lovers 33
Hands Up, Hands Down 34
Code Blue 36
Tail Wags the Dog 37

The Impossible Temper of Our Times (Part One) 38
The Impossible Temper of Our Times (Part Two) 40

Part Four: Double Helix 41

Eleven Eleven Eleven Twelve 42
Go Leafs Go 44
Motivation 47
Geologia Hominum Huius Temporis 48
Forgiveness 50
Self-Invention (One) 52
Reinvention (Two) 54
Reinvention (Three) 56
Reinvention (Four) 58
Not So Little Brother and His Insatiable Appetite for Life 60
Remembering Russell 65

Part Five: Soapbox Sermonettes 71

So Much, So Little 72
Look 73
How Are You? Thanks for Asking 74
Rallying Cry 76
Conquistadors 78
Power Up & Down 81
Maybe I've Got This Wrong 83
Binary Code 84
The Non-Secrets of Life (Part One): Work, Failure: Gravity, Balance 86
The Non-Secrets of Life (Part Two): Coming to Terms 88
The Non-Secrets of Life (Part Three): Time Time Time 89

Part Six: Time Time Time 91

When Time Is Beautiful 92
When Time Is Ugly 93
The Future in The Present: A Change in the Weather 95
The Present Can Be a Gift 97

Part Seven: Ars Nova 2020 99

Do Heals Make Noise? 100
Txtng 101
Like 102
The World of Song 104
Ultra-Talk! 105
Snowflakes 107
Dream #23,475 109
Oh Canada 110

Grateful Acknowledgements 111

Preface — Recreational Therapy

Dinner, July 2010.
My son B-man said — write a book.
Chapter on politics, one on religion,
things that enliven the dinner table.
Plants a bucket-list seed.
My wife Jeannette (she's a real pip) always said — *write a book.*
Some of my high school English teachers thought
I might turn into a writer.
My physiotherapist Eldon has told me many times
(as we yack, and he cracks my back):
"Natural storyteller. *Write a book.*"
So — okay.
The concept of autobiography as *poetry* is inspiring —
the process enjoyable.
Free-verse forms, like Ultra-Talk,
liberate the project from rulebooks, historic structure.
Here's a medium
to address the percolating head,
pour it out
into spiral notebooks.

Just give yourself permission.

So I did.

Cheers,

R

THE HUMANITIES

The Search Is Sacred

So much human blood sweat & tears
devoted to the supernatural,
the metaphysical —
cathedrals built for gods and kings,
prayers to ancestors, hymns that ring.
Imagination conjures
an afterlife:
figments of evolutionary networking
from the frontal cortex to the parietal & temporal lobes.
Homo habilis > erectus > sapiens:
This problem-solver needs an answer, and

God answers everything.

Leave us
to construct byzantine puzzles of words
to feed a hunger
that no broker or banker could satisfy.
Strike up the cosmic music
that encourages spirits to dance from lobe to lobe to lobe.

Now, astronomers and astrophysicists explore the universe.
They find black holes,
discover any number of things
deadly to puny earthlings.
Alas: no evidence
of any heavenly kingdom to come.

Nothing is sacred: except, perhaps
rigorous applications of scientific method:
the undeniable logic of pure mathematics:
the beautiful mind of Da Vinci:

the architecture of Bach:
Newton: Darwin: Edison: Einstein:
ohhh, the symmetrical poetics of
the veining
from the petriole and midrib of the maple leaf . . .

Well, all right:
anything is sacred
that sparks a search
for answers.

These Be the Attitudes

Let's consider the conundrums of virtuous liberality.

Blessed are the tolerant: for they must endure
the stupid and the ignorant.
Blessed are the meek: for they shall get railroaded
by rapacious profiteers.
Blessed are the humble, and the patient:
for they must suffer the rude, belligerent braggarts & bullies.
Blessed are the merciful and the forgiving:
for, somehow, they can rationalize
the criminally insane, the perverse,
the unrepentant sociopaths and the misanthropes.
Blessed are the pacifists, for turning their other cheek to
the anarchists and the mass shooters.
Blessed are the peacemakers, for they will be
manipulated, exploited, then
written off as collateral damage by the warmongers.

It's rugged individualism.
Trickle-down economics.
It's scattershot patterns of blood splatter
from dogs eating dogs.
It's culture-creep evil
from delusional psychos,
oil & gas & gun lobbyists and
Dark Money.

Winners take what they want,
feelin' all justified & mighty righteous,
whatever the cost.
They don't give a shit
about consequences.

So — blessed are the losers
for their thoughtful deference
facilitates their own conquest & subjugation.

And the winners use blessings
as opiates for the masses
for this is the way of the world
as they proclaim —

We've done NOTHING wrong.

Self-Confession: Uncommonly Reasonable Secular Agnostic Common Prayer

Almighty Universe, Mother Nature,
(Can I call you Gaia? I'd like to call you Gaia),
Comprehensive Matrix of Physics & Chemistry & Biology,
Maker of All Things:
Singular Reality Yet Infinite Mystery to All Human Beings:

I acknowledge and confess my manifold sins,
which, from time to time, I have committed
(and likely will continue to commit) by thought, word and deed,
against common sense, rational thought and
the general welfare of humanity.

I am, frankly, embarrassed
by my frail and fallible
rationalizations of your boundless eternity.

I do earnestly repent, and am heartily sorry for these misdoings —
these transgressions: this
selfish, stupid, ill-conceived, rash, judgmental, ignorant and
petty misconduct.

My bad.

I'm wondering if you can give me a break . . . ?
A merciful moment
within your wondrous yet
totally neutral, disinterested, infinitely random chaos;
for the sake of my ancestors, my loved ones, my friends,
neighbours, acquaintances, complete strangers,
as well as my children's children's children:

Allow me an opportunity to forgive myself all that is past
And grant that I may ever hereafter
Serve and please others in newness of life
To the honour and glory of secular pluralistic humanist reason
Through a filter of benevolent courtesy and gracious virtue

AMEN.

Angels

Michelangelo saw
the angel in the stone.
Adam Sol says
some poets see
the aardvark in the angel.
And the ant is in the aardvark, and
Adam's in the ant.

There's an angel in the Adam —
in the aardvark.
In the ant.

There are angels in the architecture —
that's what Simon says.
There's always something more
than meets the eye.

It's
the movement that's divine
and according to Sol
some poets see

the angels in it all.

Love Is the Answer

What if matter
didn't matter anymore?
What if reality came to an end?

"Space" goes on, forever and ever, amen.
Contemplating the infinite — the eternal — is
terrifying / intriguing / perplexing and confounding.
It defies and escapes us: stretches beyond us:
turns a feeble little mind into
a modest mush of contradictions, fears, insignificance.

The fallback, default position — a zone of comfort,
for the meek and humble —
is that love is the answer to the infinite questions.
In this existence, Love is the highest purpose that we can imagine.

            I am alone.

So very separate and detached.
Fraught with contradictions and weakness, prone to mistakes and errors.
Yet I am also husband and father, son and brother,
the most important roles of my life —
more of a team-type role player than a rogue entity.
Still — I vacillate between family member and individual —
trying to balance the need to belong
with the longing to be free.
The best "default" mode is
one of loving, caring,
tenderness and forgiveness —
because that's the best way to deal
with our very human tendencies
towards inconsistency and blundering glitches.

Glundering blitches.
Wondering bitches.
Wandering itches.
Pondering riches.

Ashes will scatter
the proof of the matter
Blood is the dancer and
Love is the answer.

LIFE
AND
DEATH

Have a Good Day

Hey, kids. Let me spell this out for you.
Once you've worked the rodeo for a while,
you catch the general drift.
You can plainly see where this is going.
Not exactly blowing up the news cycle here:
in fact, this is pretty much common as dirt.

Here's how this all plays out.

Child becomes father to the man.
(Thanks, Wordsworth.)
Geezer reverts to helpless infant
and there's precious little poetry to be found there.
If you're lucky enough to survive middle age,
the brain tires quickly —
it cannot maintain the thread —
it cannot easily conjure nor grasp *La Grande Ligne.*
The aches of the body become a distraction —
then overpower —
then extinguish
life's pleasures.

First there will be
a loss of mobility and independence
then a loss of faculties
then of reason.

Then, propped up in a hospice bed (hey, brothers!),
or flat out on a gurney in an overcrowded ER, with
intubation coming out of your mouth (hiya, Mom!) (hey, Nana!);
or sitting in a chair in your sister's hallway (there's Grandpa!),
you get to return to the oblivion from
whence you emerged.

Sound like a plan? You got it.
So?
So — be kind.
Have fun.
And have a good day.

Dear Diary

July 2007

Dear Diary: turned 54 today
a little overwhelmed by love along the way.
Make a wish, blow out the candles, claim it's
all a piece of cake, and then I'll turn the page, Dear Diary.

Dear Diary: my blessing is my curse.
I love my crazy life so much it hurts.
Headed downhill, past my prime,
but less obsessed with marking time,
so turn the page, Dear Diary.

I write down all my mysteries here,
and hope some lines of verse appear,
cuz what comes pouring out
gets me through somehow.
Another year of words
came spilling from my pen,
yesterdays compiled and consigned to there and then
whatever helps to keep me here and now — (here and now)
Dear Diary: in our own strange way of things,
only you and I will know the secret promises
that each tomorrow brings.

Game Changer

In memory of Gord Downie

In the summer of 2016
Gord Downie went supernova.
The shield of the dominion cracked open.
The sleeping giant awoke
in thermals of heat and light.

From beer league hosers in their flannel
to undergrads getting baked on blunts at cottage lakes
he offered a book of common verse.

Then
when
fate began
to force his hand
he anteed up
and raised the stakes —
a moving target of courage,
defying the grip of harsh mortality.
He strutted:
he sang, *This is how it's done.*
He raged into the face of death.
Hearts breaking, the landscape
altered by thought, word and deed.

He was us.
And we were his.

No poet of ours ever dreamed as big.
No rock star class clown ever danced a better jig.
Dream catcher. Game changer. Netminder. Spellbinder.

The raven swooped low
across his path
and stuck a trickster's feather
in his cap.

Never before had we seen his kind.
And it's hard to see
how these things could ever be
the same old same old
again.

Four Stanzas

The spring of youth brings searing
awareness of infinities
the dawning of eternal mysteries
the promise of tomorrows that will
reveal and enrich
with flavours that explode
as bold emotions test control

And then
summer blooms immortal
full of cocky crowning glories
ever-present
never-ending hours of daylight
accommodate siestas
as the constellations align

Then autumn turns brown
fades green to rust
there's something in the air
that smells of the soil
hints of death
calling
say your goodbyes
make your peace
as realities gradually settle in

Then winter descends upon us
there's shrinkage in the bitter cold
long tenebrous nights begrudgingly yield
to short, dull, grey days.
The creaking in our limbs
painfully reminds us

of how little we have grown
how much remains unknown
and still there is this longing
for the turning of the wheel, the
spin around the sun
orbits in the circles
in the circles
in the circles
in the

Ticket to Ride

My father is aging
slowly disintegrating
in wearisome descent for a few decades —
losing mobility and dignity
nobility, then
reason
and memory

fading.

Those who bear witness
mourn the decline of the flesh
and the next in line
will inherit
the ticket to ride,
that long pernicious slide
into oblivion.

I could exhort him to not go gently,
show some rage
but he would never have understood the reference.
Besides, only *suppressed* emotion
is in his nature.
I would pray for him
but he and I, we have no gods
in heaven or in hell.

I could hope for the transition to be painless
dignified and peaceful
but our bodies do not always respond to our minds —
they have a stubbornness all their own.

My god is the word, in the music, in the arts,
so I will pray with my work
for him
for me
for us.

Loss, Grief, Ritual

Loss

The depth of our sadness resonates
in empty space
because we had the joy of our knowing
the full truth of love —
the wisdom of our emotion.

Grief

This is what it feels like
to be human —
to become aware of the size of goodness
and the weight of our shortcomings.

Ritual

Light a candle.
Put it in the window
of your dark house
so the world can see it
glimmer with hope.
Share yours
with ours.

Born to Pay

There's an old man in the mirror
gaining on me fast.
His claim upon the future
overtakes our glorious past.
And when it's comin' down to him or me
it'll all work out okay
'cause we both know the price
that we were born to pay.

When I was just a boy —
full of promise — green & tender
I took so much for granted
no accounting for surrender.
But now the changes come so fast
at the speed of light they say
now that's the price
every child is born to pay.

Oh, devil at each crossroad
Angel in my ear
Should I turn to face the music?
Learn the language that I hear?
Should I wager all & let it ride?
Or fold this hand I hold and walk away?

There's a sobering reflection
I've grown to recognize
the telltale signs of showbiz lines
from a master of disguise
But it looks like he's still game
with one more round to play
he'll ante up
the price he's born to pay.

He knows I'm good to cough the damage
each & ev'ry day
'cause we both know the price
that we were born to pay
yeah, we both know
that we were born to pay.

Definitions, Perspective and Choices

Kierkegaard said
Man is spirit.
But what is spirit?
Spirit is the self.
But what is the self?
Man is a synthesis of the infinite and the finite,
of the temporal and the eternal . . .

Well — can't buy in.
The imagination can contemplate the eternal —
but K's "spirit" sounds a lot like ego.
And once the imagination in a brain stops functioning,
the self / ego / spirit / eternal is *done.*
While the brain is still working
you, yourself, are ever-changing,
synthesizing, morphing, evolving, adapting.
But the brain is mortal.
Mortality is the thing that makes sense to me.
And when your sense / senses are done,
you are done.

Questions, perspectives
need to be tempered —
bounded by their impermanence.
"You" are finite.

And common.
A grain of sand on a beach, on a planet filled with beaches,
in a universe with planets in about 200 billion galaxies:
that's something like 1,000,000,000,000,000,000,000,000 — 10^{24}
— planets
in the observable Universe.

That's an unimaginable number of sandy beaches.
(Let's not get into black holes.)

Feeling small & insignificant?
Let's not forget old Thomas Hobbes, with his take on life:
"Solitary, poor, nasty, brutish and short."
Yes, yes.
But — still — here "you" are, for your wee brave tango.

So on to Socrates, and the principle of *examination.*

The Examined Life Is Worth Living

Simon Critchley offers:
be in the world —
don't think, look —
turn outwards not inwards —
observe closely and switch off your doubts.

So — for now — *for this precious moment* —
let's just go with Richard Branson (and Nike):
"Screw it — let's do it. Just get on with it and do it."

Because it may only be a tiny window of opportunity, but
you might as well *dance*.
And man's spirit — his solitary, poor, nasty, brutish and short spirit —
requires goodness.
Virtue.
And even when something bad happens along —
it either destroys, defines or strengthens.
So even out of the negative, you can choose the positive.

So it's in the *choosing*.
Not the defaulting: the instinctive knee-jerking.

Choices.

Courage of Convictions

Instinct offers clues
What do you think?
What do you feel?
But then the process leads to something stronger, deeper,
more fully realized.
What do you *know*?
What do you *believe*?

And if you can find the answers to those questions, then
that's "conviction,"
more firmly held.

Still: this will never be enough.
For what are you prepared to *DO*,
based on the belief you firmly hold?
How will you *ACT*?
Action speaks louder than words —
action requires courage.

The courage of conviction
is a muscle that requires daily exercise.

You must act, behave, according to your beliefs.

This is so you can look yourself straight in the eye in the mirror
and think — You're ok — you did what you could.
Sleep well, old friend.

In the early going, this "courage" might be hard to muster,
but after a while, after the muscles of conviction are in good shape,
it can come quite naturally, and it doesn't feel
"courageous" or "brave" at all.

It's just standard operating procedure.

Of course — then — how often will you stop and ask yourself,
What if I'm wrong about this?
Because you always have to allow
that you could be mistaken.
And it takes courage to question,
courage to change.
It takes courage to admit that
your convictions never give you divine entitlement
to swing a sword of righteousness.

The golden rule, the courage to be humble.
Modest. Reasonable.
Can you find the courage
to become committed to that?

THERE'S POLITICS IN EVERYTHING

There's Politics in Everything

Once upon an ancient time
I was moderating a debate in a college classroom
and as emotions rose a bit
I tried to sound professorial
and said,

Let's try to leave politics out of the discussion.

And a young woman looked at me
like I had grown an extra head —
or lost the one I thought I had.

And she said,

You can't leave politics out of anything.
Politics is IN everything.

And the more I've thought about it
& thought about it
& still think about it

the more I believe

she was absolutely right.

Genders Strangers Foreigners Lovers

Impossible to argue
over half-empty glasses at two minutes to midnight.
It's true — our world is an unholy mess.

No chromosome ever offered immunity
from loss, hurt, sickness, despair, heartache, grief,
injury, disappointment and disillusion.
Life takes it out on every strand in the gene pool
and beats down harder
on the short straws
in the shallow end.

After all, we are so often
strangers to ourselves
as much as we are
foreign to each other.

Yet . . .

I do know this.
I am never so complete
as when I am fully engaged
surrendered
willingly committed
in the service of others.

Hands Up, Hands Down

Hands up, those who have questions.

Hands up, those who feel like the dream of democracy
has turned toxic.

Hands up, those who feel like
you've been robbed & jobbed
by lowlife hijackers and snake-oil carpetbaggers.

Show of hands, please, from
those who are volunteering to fight against
mercenary warlords, corporate profiteers and corrupt politicians.

Hands up, those who vote to oppose the motion
down the poisonous slippery slope
towards the decline & fall.

Hands up, those who instinctively
seek to shield their faces
from the constant onslaught.

Hands up, those who surrender.

But our hands! Our hands are tied.
The complexity of the human world has us tangled
in an infinite braid of byzantine Gordian Knots.
And even if we managed to

free ourselves

we'd be left with a chaotic pile of
weft and warp,

strings and fibres,
threads and strands.

How would we ever come to terms
with that incomprehensible mess?

It's got us defeated,
hands down.

Code Blue

A liberal democracy
used to insist
on the rule of law.
It was essential that law enforcement
remain separate from politics.

Not anymore.

Nothing is separate from partisan politics anymore.

The cracks and divides are widening.
You can smell the gangrene
from the Civil War.

The climate is in critical condition.
Culture is toxic.
Walls are up:
lines are down.
The systems are broken.
The patient is in stage four.

Who cares?
Cuz what's on the agenda
is power to the party
and hail to the chief —
autocratic tyrant
total totalitarian.

Beat a hasty, full retreat
into your silos.

Tail Wags the Dog

It's a world of spin doctors:
handlers: media consultants: publicists:
managers of managers of managers.
The tail wags the dog and has been doing it for so long now
there really isn't any dog to speak of anymore.
Everything that goes public
is geared towards life support for the tail.

There used to be a political "system," and the media covered it.
Now politics is a snake pit of dysfunction
and the media systematically gets in our face.

McLuhan was an oracle.
The medium is the message:
the media covers the media,
and analyzes their own coverage.
And who owns the media?
The telecoms, the multinational conglomerates,
the Four Horsemen of Technology and their corporate minions.
It's a miracle if anything approaching reality,
anything approaching real work,
or real solid social contract activity,
actually gets accomplished, or even exposed,
once the digital universe has assimilated the "information."
Public Service has been polluted by Public Relations.
Journalism struggles (and increasingly fails)
against the prevailing global social conditions dictated by technology:
return a profit to the shareholders
of a very small division
of your media conglomerate corporation's
bottom line.

The bottom line is all *tail.*

The Impossible Temper of Our Times (Part One)

So — this is how winning has become losing.

In 1964, Marshall McLuhan wrote that "The Medium Is the Message."
In 1985, Neil Postman wrote that we are "Amusing Ourselves to Death."
In 2016, Americans elected a reality TV star as the POTUS.

Cheeto Trumpelthinskin is all about sloganeering —
his vainglorious obsession with "winning" dangerously shallow games.

Not to rain on capitalism's Victory Parades, but
just to cast a bit of historical sunlight
on how the gerrymandering of wealth / winning works
for the haves, and the consequences that accrue to the have-nots:
heads might roll.

Over on the Right, the Righteous believe they're "winning."
As "messages" trend towards meaninglessness,
media (and there's no "medium" in any "medium")
plays to the entrenched.
Donny the Bully Twittler brays about "fake news,"
but truth was always a casualty of his culture.
The whole wide world has been steadily losing.
America is fractured apart,
divided by partisan practices of fear and division.
There's a Death Valley depth between Left and Right, rich and poor.

Over on the Right, the Righteous believe
they're justified, sanctified, virtuous.
Why in heaven's name would they align
with the Twitter-Fingered Cheeto,
a cartoon character who is a charlatan: pretender: immoral, unethical,
venal, lying, rude, crude, uncivil, unkind, insulting?

The moral hypocrisy is baffling.

Because,

What would Jesus do?
Well — he threw the moneylenders out of the temple:
shared kindness and humility with little children:
forgave prostitutes and was hands-on with lepers:
told the parable of the Good Samaritan.

The POTUS, given to insults, would call someone like that a *Loser*.
Perpetually self-congratulatory, of course, he defines himself as a
Winner.
This is the tone set for the free world.
And an awful lot of you folks keep buyin' in.

What's WITH that?

The Impossible Temper of Our Times (Part Two)

No: true paladins figure out
that someone has to champion the downtrodden,
the weak, the lame, the sick, the poor.

Bring us your huddled masses.
There used to be a Lady Liberty who stood for those values.
Where has she gone?
Where is her lamp beside her golden door?

She's been forgotten in the dog-eat-dog Law of the Jungle.
She's been drowned out by the trumpeting elephant
threatening from the right,
across the great divide, assaulting the enemy.
The ugly noise defies comprehension:
its embrace by the MAGA base
stumps any propensity towards gracious diplomacy,
and makes reason and common sense
impossible.

DOUBLE HELIX

Eleven Eleven Eleven Twelve

Once there was a war that didn't end all wars.
My grandfather lied so he could go.
(I carry his name.)
Enflamed by the temper of the times,
dutiful boys donned the uniforms of men
and sent 20 bucks of their monthly paychecks
home to their mothers.

His record shows that once, there,
he went absent without leave
and got Field Punishment.
Shackled to a cannon? Close to No Man's Land? Under fire?
He never spoke of his tour of duty.

War obliges us to confront the enemy within and without —
immoral authority, chains of command and the evil greed for power.

On September 30, 1918, 42 days before the Boche surrendered,
they poisoned him with shell gas.
He spent two weeks stretchered at Dannes Camiers
then crossed the channel
to Eastern General Hospital in Cambridge.
41 days later he went to Casualty Clearance at Wokingham,
then they shipped him home for discharge: February 8, 1919.
His war adventure lasted 24 months.

My grandpa always smelled of cigarettes and candy mints.
He liked fancy Yardley soaps
and palm slaps of Old Spice aftershave —
maybe to mask the teenaged memory
of fetid stenches in harrowing trenches.
I remember him as a sad, burdened, earnest man

with kidney and gallstones, a bad ticker
and an arthritic invalid wife who faded away
in a Catholic chronic care hospital called Our Lady of Mercy.

In 1965, he died on a Thursday morning in November,
sitting in his coat in the front hall of his sister's house.
I was 12 years old.
He was gone: forever —
beyond knowing,
beyond thinking, beyond feeling.
His life, good, bad, indifferent, went from real to unreal:
from significance to oblivion.
Unrewarded — his passing awakened a questioning path
in my adolescent mind,
and began the erosion of my faith
in a god
in a heaven.

I can't remember what I never knew.
I can't forget
all that I will never know.

Go Leafs Go

In 1962, when the Toronto Maple Leafs won
  the first of 3 Stanley Cups in a row, I was 9.
My grandmother had two seats in the north-end blues
  at Maple Leaf Gardens.
Once a season, my dad would take me downtown
  on the west-end street cars
    for a Saturday night game.
Here, in awesome and incredibly glorious, bright colour,
was a magical world that, mostly, I only knew from the
grainy black & white TV broadcasts of Hockey Night in Canada,
which joined play in progress during the 2nd period —
the prevailing wisdom of the CBC in those days.
The Reds and Blues sections had lots of men
  in suits & ties, and fedoras:
    women in furs, teetering up & down the concrete steps
      in their high heels.
The hallways were filled with enlarged black & white photos
that showed legendary players like Babe Pratt and Syl Apps:
the intensity of Rocket Richard's eyes:
the glory of Barilko's Cup-winning goal . . .
This was the heyday of the Original Six.

As kids, we would play ball hockey out on the street, and pretend
to stickhandle with the intensity of Keon,
  shoot like Mahovlich, pass like Red Kelly
or do patented Johnny Bower split saves and poke checks,
courtesy of the images conjured in our heads via the play-by-play
of Foster ("He shoots! He scores!") Hewitt and his son Bill.

By 1967, the last time the Leafs won the Cup,
I was 13, in grade 9 at high school.

I was starting to have a deeper understanding of how life worked:
I could see that the Leafs were a 3rd place team,
with a minus-7 goal differential.
They won with aging-but-still-sometimes-superlative goalkeepers,
and defensive strategies that tested
the hooking & holding & interfering limits of referees:
shut-down wingers, shot-blocking and penalty-killing.
It was definitely the end of an era,
because the '67–68 season ushered in NHL expansion.

The Age of the Original Six was over.

Flash forward 11 years, to March of 1978.
The Massey Hall booking of the rock band I was playing in —
Triumph —
got cancelled because the venue management refused to allow our
pyrotechnics.
In a pushy career move of outrageous chutzpah,
we convinced Michael Cohl and Concert Productions International
to move our show to the Concert Bowl of Maple Leaf Gardens.
On the afternoon of Tuesday, March 21,
a limo drove me through the truck entrance off of Wood Street,
the north end of the venue from the south-facing façade
on Carlton at Church.
And then I got to walk out on the stage for soundcheck,
and drink in the view.
There were those north-end blues, where I'd sat as a young boy,
under the hallowed cathedral dome that Conn Smythe had built.
This place had hosted the dynasty of Teeder Kennedy,
Syl Apps and Turk Broda, which my father had told me about.
This magical building had been
the site of my own childhood dreams
of Keon, Duff, Armstrong, Horton, Baun, Brewer . . .

But tonight, this night, this place —
we had OUR name on the marquee,
and I was determined not to let this opportunity slip away.

When we came off stage, electrified with the outcome,
CPI had placed three Toronto Maple Leaf jerseys in the dressing room,
as a gift to us for the improbable success of the night.
I proudly took possession of the number 21:
Börje Salming, a fearless defender, and one of my favourite players.

Our band went on to sell out Maple Leaf Gardens
many times over the following years.
Throughout my adult life, my connection to the Maple Leafs franchise,
as with any "true" fan,
has been tested.
But one cannot deny one's DNA,
any more than one can reject the cards that Fate deals out.

When the Leafs win, all is right with the world.

Go Leafs Go.

Motivation

Why do you play?
Why do you sing?
Why do you write?

To connect into the flow of life.
Like sex.
Like fear and joy,
happiness and sadness,
balancing out and flowing like a river.

Because it's so natural
it feels supernatural.

Why?
Why *not*?
Why anything?
Why? *Because I can.*

Because I must.

Geologia Hominum Huius Temporis

March 2019

Consider the geology of a modern man.
An outside layer features tectonic plates that shift, adjust and modulate.
This **crust** fashions the masks, costumes, haircuts, etc.
And its roots can be traced back to the genetic luck of the draw,
A blend of recessive paternal grandmother and maternal grandfather.
The next inside layer is **The Upper Mantle**.
This, the thickest stratum, features a soft plasticity,
    circulating in constant motion,
trying to dissipate the convective heat rising from deep within.
Here we find the makings of a shifty ego, the wit, the class clown;
The quickness of the athlete who ran like a scared rabbit;
The singer/writer/musician/court jester/organ grinder's monkey,
conjuring strikes of heat lightning.
Drilling down: **The Lower Mantle** is deflective, protective.
We have passed through the charm that dresses the pessimism,
And now find the cynicism, sarcasm, irony, satire and stoicism
of a boy, his parents' son, adapting to the Olde World geology
    of a Man's Man.
Here, prey learns how to behave like predator.
Volcanic magma chambers can erupt in anger and fear,
Not necessarily (and beneficially) in the heat of natural play.
Deeper, we go **Hard Core**, into **The Gordian Knotting**.
The outer layers of stress and anxiety are home to unstable lava.
And finally we get to what's real: **The Inner Core**.
Here, the heat and light of three angels — Love, Faith & Hope —
wrestle five black demons —
Fear, Guilt, Shame, Inadequacy & Regret.
And we arrive at the abiding questions of **Geologia Hominum**:
How to preserve enlightenment against the darkness?
How to hold a graceful orbit,
    avoiding the degradation of gravitational pull?

How to revel in the joys of life
and not surrender to the deadening burden of knowledge,
the loss of hope & faith?
How to achieve Balance? How to untie the knots of ambition,
learn to let go of a lifetime of fight & flight from the demon shadows?
How to move beyond predator and prey?
Sometimes he thinks he knows too much for his own good. (Hubris!)
Sometimes he knows he feels too deeply
    for his own paltry limitations. (Crybaby!)
Consider: the physical spirituality of the cosmos.
Consider: forgiveness.
Consider: that the answer to the questions of letting go, is to Let Go.
Again. And again and again and yet again.
Let go of the gravity —
the force that holds the crust, the mantles,
let go of the core.
Let go.
Let
go.

Forgiveness

A river ran under a bridge
then the current weakened
and finally stopped.
No more blood, no sweat, no tears —
the bed dried up and cracked,
just a desiccated graveyard.

Then a rainy season came.
A blessed relief,
a supernatural gift
a chance for a new life.

And what is required of a truly fresh start?

Retire the cast of characters from the imaginary morality play:
The prosecuting attorney, the trial judge,
the scorekeeper —
St. Peter, Maalik and Leviathan.
Goodbye & good riddance.

Stem the flow of volcanic bile,
no longer enraging in scarlet anger,
casting monstrous shadows.
Then get out the compass and seek the virtuous path — a higher road.
Choose a pursuit of the light, and find a way out of the darkness.
To be smaller, thinner, more modest and humble
and to be good with that:
know it,
own it.

To do the work, and dig the holes deep, then
consciously decide to bury all the hatchets.

To move past the hurt, the anger, the sorrow, the betrayal,
release the demon fire that has defined your secret tortured spirit.
Let it go.
Banish the grievances.
Disown the regret.
Leave it all behind.

Then, the final tribulation —
to forgive one's self
for stubborn, foolish pride,
for the past inability to be merciful,
and in good faith,
step down
off the treadmill.

Self-Invention (One)

Clever child! So talented!
A pat on the back swells the head —
stroke of the chromosomes.

Gifts, talents:
no more of a miracle, really, than eye or hair colour:
they are simply innate.
Notes out of thin air, in the ear, in the brain, from the throat:
physical manifestations, dexterity, speed.
Quick, like a scared rabbit: the wit of a class clown.
Humble as these endowments were,
they still offered a way to play through shyness and insecurities.
One hears the calling,
as much as the avocation is making its own natural selection.
A round peg fits the round hole. Chicken < > egg.

Sympathies to those living with artists.
Caution to artists living with themselves.
The body's present, but the flow runs elsewhere:
Being here, working here; but currently, otherwise engaged.

Sondheim says Seurat
was working on the hat.
Puzzles, enigmas, cryptic crosswords,
games.

Invent the game: Invent the rules.
Invent a world you can control,
cuz you can't control the real one.

To what end?
Kilroy Was Here, carved in the wall.

(do you) hear what I hear (?)
(do you) see what I see (?)
(does it) provoke you (?) tickle your fancy (?)
(does it) give you pause to think, make you stop and feel (?)

Here's a lick. One hundred thousand licks,
woven into a tapestry — another new game.

(can you) take a torch
from the altar of the sanctuary of Hestia,
the stolen flame of Prometheus,
and pass it on?

Pass it on.

Reinvention (Two)

Picked up some street lingo
of motion and emotion
of flashing lightning speed and
soul-grinding blues.

Became a disciple of the blood lines
Kings and Johnsons
Sor, Granados, Albeniz
Chester & Lester
Eric Jeff Jimmy & Jimi.

It was a game of play
games within games
to play within a play
where mortal limitation and ego are
surrendered and lost in the moment
where human time ceased to exist
but only the current of the cosmic river
flows along.

Put the strings in my hands:
I am cocky and full of hormonal swagger,
both puppet and puppeteer.
Let my hands connect my head & my heart,
let them conjure magic out of thin air.
Let's connect the wavelengths,
immerse in the ocean's tides.

Some might say the most eloquent expression
comes without words.
So clumsy, when the notes,
against,

inside,
amongst the chords,
can be so fluent
        fluid
                flow.

Dive into the river,
feel it washing all around you —
surround you
        a round and
                around and around.

Reinvention (Three)

Of my own free will   I invented the manchild
a Rocket in cartoon costumes,
and so what if I did?
Damned cuz I did — damned if I didn't
assist in the production of
the funhouse of smoke & mirrors,
inside the grand houses of cards
that got built up all around.
Meanwhile, I proudly scrawled on the dotted line:
my name, my likeness, my ass:
signed, corporate-sealed & delivered —
property belonging to multi-purpose
vertically and horizontally integrated business enterprises.
Anything I might do or affix in any form
was a potential asset of the brands and the logos
and the divisional management suits
in those surrounding office buildings of cards.

Of my own free will — I was owned. (And I've had to own that.)

To the front of house, I was a barking seal,
an organ grinder's monkey, a clawless clueless toothless tiger,
leaping around on platforms at the crack of a whip —
the poke of a chair.

Inside the house, backstage,
I was the junior partner
who got outvoted on things that really mattered
and got managed and manipulated into much of the rest.

Why did I let it happen? What went to motivation, Your Honour?
That higher purpose was to build a marriage,

a family, a real life with the woman I love.
I wanted to manufacture the wind that would fill our sails,
the multiplying provisions of a distinct church & state.

Alas. Eventually, there was no destiny, no fate
that I felt I could call my own.
The artist I had become was not something
that the human being inside me could live with.
The Machine had lost
whatever naïve ghost of a soul it might have had.
For me — the Fun House was empty.
It did not take as much courage to walk away
as it had been costing me humanity,
sanity,
to stay.

Cue reinvention — part four.

Reinvention (Four)

So, this happened: the rise of grunge
and the fall of an arena rock / corporate house of cards
  cartoon character.
Then nine years into the inevitable transition
(for the only constant is Change),
an original muse strung in nylon invited me back to the start,
to reconnect to the sharing
of simple, humble gifts.

"Too talented for his own damn good."
Never talented enough for his own sacred yearnings.

What is the point?
In a world full of percentage points,
penetration points into demographic pie slices —
one eventually trains their courage of convictions
on the pull of their own magnetic north.

How long does it take for you to learn to trust your gut?

Shakespeare's Polonius remarks "to thine own self be true,"
but George Bernard Shaw says life isn't about finding yourself,
it's about creating yourself.
Yes.
And then recreating. And reinventing.

Ah, artists: with their Groucho Marx perversion —
refusing to belong to a club
that would have the likes of them as a member.
Organize artists? Like trying to herd cats.

Still the wheel keeps on turning
the river keeps on running
the tide keeps on ebbing and flowing
even magnetic north keeps moving.
Why, in the last 150 years, the pole has wandered about 685 miles.

So go.
Go with the motion.
Honour your humble gifts.
Respect them and do them justice.
Choose what feels sacred.
Serve others.
Strive to be virtuous.
Pass along the flame of Prometheus.
And leave the campsite better than you found it.

Not So Little Brother and His Insatiable Appetite for Life

Once upon an actual time — May of 1958 —
the amniotic fluid of a very pregnant woman
picking rhubarb in her backyard garden
bursts, and soon the Emmett boys
have a baby brother who's in a hurry
hungry to get started.

Five and a half years later, in a snowstorm,
that kid gets tobogganed back from kindergarten
with a bead stuck up his nose.
Once safely home, it simply falls out.
A few weeks later, still naturally curious,
he does it again.

Out back of 94 Abbott Avenue,
bikes and ancient lawnmowers,
3rd generation rakes, shovels and ice choppers
fill up the "storage" garage and the unheated back porch.
It's the repository for the little bro's wading pool,
tricycle and giant plastic yard toys
from the local Towers department store —
foreshadowing hockey nets and sticks, sports equipment
and trunks full of theatre props, masks and costumes.

A little older now,
sharing the back bedroom of the semi-detached house,
that kid jams a pillow down into his pyjama bottoms
when his dad comes upstairs
to administer corporal punishment via the Wooden Spoon.
A few spanks through the covers, a few whimpers of mock agony,
and two brothers start laughing so hard
it drains the imperative right out of the patriarch — forever.

Once upon another evening,
three brothers sit on their parents' bed
watching the black & white portable TV
  inherited from Grandpa Gord,
enjoying an episode of *Hogan's Heroes.*
Little Bro wonders out loud
why mysterious things start happening to his own body
 when the Colonel is necking with a dishy blonde German *frau.*
Ahhhh — good times.

Captured alive in photos, walking the beaches of the Maritimes.
Get a good look: this kid has a lust for life,
a joy of Being in the Moment.
Little brothers have a lot to teach their elders.
That kid somehow brings home his teacher,
a stray, a gay ceramic potter and his cooking
and his Siamese and Burmese cats,
into a '70s show TV sitcom experiment,
where narrow, sheltered middle-class family values
learn to embrace the lonely identity search
of a gentle man from an alternative lifestyle.

Cut to a gangly kid in lacrosse gear,
getting hacked, whacked and pounded
in an outdoor rink at Campbell Park, just off Wallace Avenue.
That kid is struggling with the difference between
macho and just plain stupid,
partly because he is a Little Bro,
always trying to prove that he deserves to hang with the Big Boys,
needing just a bit more courage and dogged determination:
in the touch football games at Oakmount Park,
and epic neighbourhood street hockey tournaments
at Indian Road Crescent Public School.

This is a quasi-religious coming-of-age activity,
a ritual of stinky gloves and musty pads,
with homemade Ken-Dryden-styled goalie masks
fashioned from wire hangers, paper maché and masking tape.

Who is that teenager, getting himself in a hot pot spot of trouble
  in a high school stairwell?
Who paints that YES logo on the oil tank
  in the perpetually damp basement, and *why?*

When did the Parade of Girlfriends begin?
For it is surely a long and glorious procession.

Impossible to tie down the guy
who drives the parts wagon for Uncle Ken:
the guy who moves out of his parent's house
to live in a 3rd floor walk-up with Korky,
about a block away from his mom & dad:
the guy who sets a new record for deliveries as a Canpar driver
but in the process also unfortunately
breaks the old mark for accidents, and gets fired:
that reckless guy, hell-bent for a good time,
who can't learn to say "no" to anyone:
who lives in a bungalow basement flat
on Grandville Avenue in early '78
and survives a spring flood,
then takes his motorcycle apart
into a thousand pieces out in the garage
spreading it halfway up the driveway.

There is no pigeon-holing
of the Tortus Wynd Theatre Company founding partner,
and no accounting for some hellhole of a shared apartment

down by St. Joe's Hospital.
Along comes the Skelton Road era —
the Dream Police, the whippets, the Car Business,
Terry's late-night visits (before he becomes Terence):
Peter Perry and "*Bic*,"
Halloween horror shows
with Zachariah *from the war-torn battlefields of China!*
Murphy's British adventure,
with our hero posing as the Canadian shuffleboard champion
who has lost his touch under the influence of Guinness:
hitting golf balls poorly in Scotland,
but leaving bananas for the bin-men . . .

Ballbusters become Roosties become Cadillacs
and a championship arrives —
Rusty Cleats enjoy glorious seasons in Mississauga parks,
chucking Red Dots around
like rotator cuffs & knees & fingertips can last forever.
He says one of the most beautiful things in life is a stand-up triple.
He should know — he gets his fair share.
The Liar's Club came and went,
but the reign of the King of the Credit Woodlands is secure,
and his legendary role as Party Host Extraordinaire
and Best Guest Ever is guaranteed.

Who could break a toe by catching it in a backyard volleyball net?
Who puts his Christmas gift underwear on over his pants,
then proudly poses for the photo op?
On a Christmas Day, who lies down on the upstairs landing rug
and catches sock balls in his mouth,
tossed by his giggling twin nieces
when he's too pooped to even stand up?

But then — who stood tall before me in our kitchen
and tried to be supportive, gentle and caring
as he told us that the dark spot on his liver was malignant?
Who kept his courage and his determination, battling impossible odds
fighting cancer like a tiger
with his sense of humour and his Lust for Life intact?
On the day I took him to the hospital for the chemo session
when they told him his deteriorating blood
disqualified him from further treatment,
who stopped to smile and enjoy the tropical fish in the aquarium?
Who went over to enthusiastically join the crowd in its ovation
for a successful patient who got to ring the Finish Bell?

That's the guy I remember —
the little brother who will always have something to teach me.

Remembering Russell

My younger brother's cancer diagnosis
was April of 2006.
After that, I can't recall the timeline, anymore —
the downhill blur of tests, surgeries, chemo,
the desperate research,
the terrified pinning of faint hope to quack cures
the subcutaneous implant
to buy time.

I remember being with Russ
out in a canoe on a Muskoka lake
so conflicted: happy to be sharing the moment
making the memory
yet simultaneously so sad and heartbroken
because we both knew this was likely
our last good time together —
the final act
in his last brave performance for me.

I remember the jaundice.
How the strong, tall, athletic body,
of which he had made so many demands
over four decades,
had finally betrayed him.
I remember the heart-to-hearts
and the one when he turned the tables on me —
instead of addressing the order of his own affairs,
he stunned me with a dying wish —
a sincere request to clean up my own act
unload my own burdens
work my way towards forgiveness
make peace
seek higher purpose.

I remember hugging him —
his bony skeleton
protruding through sagging waxy skin —
holding him in his despair,
when he realized the fight was finally over.
I remember feeling so empty and phony
trying to find something
anything
that might sound
like the right thing to say;
counselling him about the maintenance of dignity,
and his legendary sense of good humour
down the final stretch.
We were crying.
Don't let cancer strip away everything, I said.
He whispered,
I'll never get to walk my daughter down the aisle.

Those words will always bounce around
at the edge of a black hole in my heart.

He died in September of 2007,
wafting in and out of a morphine cloud.
I can recall some of the funeral,
snapshots in my memory bank:
then, spreading some of his ashes
on the softball diamond where
we had won a league championship.
I remember the struggles
of trying to let him go.
Taking a sandwich bag of his remains
to Sölvesborg, Sweden:
spreading some in a waterfall pond
in the hot stillness of a beautiful park

on the sunny morning of June 7, 2008:
then, later, a private ritual —
placing the rest of the grey dust,
with its tiny chips of bones and teeth
under the stage, before we went on
to play the big triumphant reunion gig.
We were there because of him,
because he'd asked me to find it
within myself.

I mixed some of what was left of him
into the concrete footings
of our three front yard light poles.
Every nightfall, the illumination kicks in,
and I think of Russell.
And some of him stays
on the mantel of my studio
in a little wooden tea box with a brass elephant on the lid
under the base of my Hall of Fame statuette
which I would never have been awarded
if it wasn't for him.

There were many years of regret over my impotence;
helplessness in the face of sorrow
my inability to save him
my failure to forgive myself.
More than a decade of survivor guilt.

But his living legacy still works on me,
pushing me along the winding path
of trying to become a better man.
Sadness has mellowed beyond regret
moving towards acceptance
of hard-won understanding.

There was great loss, but he's not lost,
because there's this, which I feel in my bones:
when you've known the technicolour radiance
of someone whose love of living was larger than life
then watched it stolen and snuffed out,
without mercy or pity,
some of that innocent illumination is gone forever.
But memory still sees it, flickering in the past.
Black becomes the most sensible colour
because you want to blend in on the long road back
from the grey shadows of twilight in a half-dream world
where sorrow has established permanence.

The age of reason had been altered
into an age of survival.
But then surviving evolved into living well, the best revenge,
because I wasn't going to let sorrow steal everything.
I will always owe it to him
to work my way back
towards his technicolour radiance.

Time has gradually, finally
shifted my take on all this.
I no longer struggle to try and let him go.
Instead — I hold his memory closer.
I welcome every opportunity to honour his legacy.
Now, I'm glad to carry him within me
have his life influencing mine
weighing my choices upon the scales of benefit & loss,
joy & sorrow, love & grief, unconscious, naïve innocence,
blind faith & guilt.
I accept that I'll always mourn
the loss of his companionship, fellowship, brotherhood.
But at least I had it — I know what it felt like.

And with every passing year, I get better with that.
I type out these words, and still
grief rises up.
But I know it's just a passing cloud, blocking the light —
and I have relearned how to trust
the warmth of that sun.

SOAPBOX SERMONETTES

So Much, So Little

Who lays claim
to this Digital Universe?
Could it be this Brave New World's
blessing, or its curse?
Presumptions and assumptions hold
that content reigns as king — but
who might seek to challenge
the destruction it can bring?

So much information, so little understanding
So much choice, so little comprehension
So much opinion, so little wisdom
So much talk, so little articulation
So much rhetoric, so little fact
So much argument, so little tact.

So much entitlement, so little commitment
So much acquisition, so little contentment
So much expectation, so little quality
So much propaganda, so little honesty
So much calculation, so little charity
So much egotism, so little humility.

So much cynicism, so little faith
So much profiteering, so little fair trade
So much complaining, so little enterprise
So much hardball, so little compromise
So much touching base, so little interface
So much judgment, so little grace.

So much competition, evil eyes gone blind
So little forgiveness, so little peace of mind.

Look

Look — up in the sky!
The carbon and the methane vultures are circling.

Harbingers of suffocation.

Look down!
The cockroaches are inheriting the earth.

Look! Over there in the parking lot!
Dogs are eating dogs.

Look around us — the walls are closing in
look back there — the past is gaining on you.

Look within:
fear, intolerance and stress.
It's *killing* you.

The vultures and the cockroaches and the dogs
are counting on it.

Look up look down
look back look around
look over look in.
Look sharp: look again.

Look again, for Gaia's sake,
look again.

Look out . . .

How Are You? Thanks for Asking

How am I doing?
Truth be told?
You'll regret asking the question.

Because I *could* say it's past the time for niceties,
for social grace & civility.
We're all getting fucked over constantly
by anyone who can,
starting from Captain Chaos von Clownstick
on down.

Our world is going to hell in a handcart.
Our digital universe frags and defrags
and destabilizes
in the access-to-information age, which
has empowered legions of the willfully misguided,
unenlightened,
undiscerning
pinheads.

How am I? *Really?*

Well — I'm too old for this shit.
I've seen and heard too much for my own good.
Lost respect for social filters.
No longer trust the *common* man
to have any *common* sense.

But what's the use?
Why *ever* say what I *could* say?
What'd be the point of even *going* there?
It's hopeless.

Besides — you'd probably say,
"Whoa, dude. Only being polite, showing a little courtesy."

So instead, I'll just respond —
I'm fine, thanks. And you? Alright. Cool.
Well — have a good day.

How am I?
Empty. Hollow.
A phony, in a phony world, full of phonies.

Thanks for asking.

Rallying Cry

Seems like
the constant evil hunger of the zeitgeist
devours the innocent
and cuts down tall poppies:
loves to take headshots at those
daring to stick their brave necks out.
The monster thrives & feasts upon
the adrenalin & cortisol of
Fight or Flight or Freeze.
The demon is addicted.
It loves a dirty fight —
the dirtier the better.
It feeds on feces
and the malice grows.
But
there's also a good fight — a clean fight — a fair fight
where choices honour the best parts of
one's self. One self. Oneself.
But that little item never cracks the news cycle,
cuz it doesn't bleed, so it doesn't lead.
But — it's an antidote.
And then, oh,
there's the flight paths of the human spirit.
Does the horizon beckon, or intimidate?
Flight runs a gamut,
from curiosity, and the courage of convictions,
reaching for higher common denominators —
all the way on down to cowardice.
Fear.
How much fear?
Because — there's the kind of fear that makes us run, and then

there's the kind of fear that freezes prey under the predator's gaze.
Now —
just — hold that thought, and say cheese for a selfie.
Hmm.
Lookin' a little
like a deer in the headlights.
Anyway . . .
We *could* fight the unconsciousness.
We could take flight,
escape the poison grasp.

We could use our fear to fly.
Rise up,
up,
above & beyond.

Conquistadors

Sir Edmund Hillary famously said
It's not the mountain we conquer but ourselves.
And on the face of it, he's saying:
Conquer your fear — conquer your self-imposed limitations.
Self-help words to live by, no doubt.
Ok.

But — in truth, in reality,
Most of us don't find the inner OR outer strength to conquer
  mountains, do we?
Most of us struggle just to come to terms with molehills.
We circumnavigate the bumps, the freckles, the warts, the pimples.
We bypass the exercise bike on the way to the cookie jar:
we don't even really summon questions of self-discipline.
We watch TV. We eat our rationalized, justified desserts.
We simply let it slide,
let it slide.
We give in to temptation,
We give in.

And what if Sir Edmund's use of the collective pronoun
unintentionally bullies us circumnavigating circumlocutionists?
What if the brave, famous mountaineer is subtly encouraging us
to beat ourselves up?

What if conquering ourselves is a gateway drug?
Like — what if "conquering" actually starts the slide
into an evil kind of psychotic delusion?

Would it still be alright if we weren't encouraging conquest?
Because — one doesn't need to look too far
to find plenty of acolytes & disciples of ancient notions.

For example, holy warrior jihadists
who crash hijacked airplanes into buildings —
self-disciplined mountaineers, conquering themselves, to be sure —
investing in an imagined Paradise of the Hereafter:
Kingdoms to Come.
No heaven on earth for these self-conquerers, after all:
this mortal coil is for discipline, self-denial, prostration — violence:
a theatre for fighters who go further.
They imagine they have become what they believe, so
they must *conquer* infidels who lack faith in the Only Truth.
Once they've *conquered* themselves,
they take the fight to those
  who don't agree with their mountaineering.
Crusaders: Conquistadors: Evangelicals:
they see infidels who require subjugation.
Mountaineers, conquering dissenting views
on topographic realities. Hoo haw.

And even though the Lord's Prayer asks for it,
none of us ever get delivered from evil, do we?
Evil conquers its own limitations, then gets out and abroad,
conquering other people's mountains.
This power of conquest spreads itself around.
It shows up at l'École Polytechnique,
the World Trade Center, Oklahoma City, the Boston Marathon,
a country music festival in Las Vegas . . .
We could go on — and on and on.
And oh, we do. We do.
And what of the human ambition to conquer nature?
The arrogant words of a one & only "god":
Let us make man in our image, after our likeness:
and let them have dominion over the fish of the sea,
and over the fowl of the air,
and over the cattle,

and over all the earth,
and over every creeping thing
that creepeth upon the earth.

Yeah, that's creepy.

We don't just *conquer* the mountains,
we exercise our *dominion.*
We pollute the sky and water
and poison the soil.
We rape and pillage the oceans:
we *plunder* this world.

So let's get to the point.

To potential Conquistadors of all stripes:
can we please forget this shit about conquering?
It's overrated.
Please consider tolerating
and adopting different mountains.
Cuz it's not just mountains we must accept:
it's ourselves.

Power Up & Down

We all enjoy the same freedom
exercised by
tinkers and tailors and soldiers and sailors
trolls and bakers, claim holders and failures
nurses and teachers and admin assistants
robots and crackpots who've joined the resistance
doctors and lawyers, firefighters and waiters
plumbers and sales reps and smooth operators.

As of this writing,
every minute, over 380 new websites go online.
Power Up!
— democracy in action, writ bold, to be sure.
So many little wars of words and
big sloppy noisy epidemics —
tempests in digital teacups.

I worship the word:
but so many get wasted:
devalued.
Stupidity & ignorance,
obscuring words that might matter.
Of course,

Everyone is entitled to a point of view, and
everyone is entitled to their passion.

And "campaigns" are all about staying on message — just the right one
flowing through as many portals & outlets as one can manage to reach.
In the Mighty Digital Universe, countless marketing worlds are
about p.r. & promo.
And as we all know,

even more than ever before —
it's about Money.
And Money is power.

Money invests in charisma: father figures reading teleprompters
from their podiums.
Cultural lifestyle icons from the mythical Land of Kardasia, etc.

Everyone's got an agenda.

We can also have ours.

Power? Power *down.*

Let's just turn the shit off.

Maybe I've Got This Wrong

A sports columnist in the daily paper wrote,
"Cheating will never be eliminated. Nor should we want it to."

That's no royal "we."
Anyone else insulted by the assumption of the collective pronoun?
Speaking for everyone, are we?

Maybe that's a bit weak, lazy, bad — *just like cheating.*

But — maybe this is simply Journalism 102,
  intentional provocation.
Perhaps what begins as healthy skepticism
sours into unhealthy cynicism, and
sarcasm curdles into misanthropy.
Jaded, our correspondent joins the Cheaters
and heads on over to the Dark Side.
Slightly perverse, slightly evil, because "slightly" is *entertaining.*
The devil has all the best tunes,
and who even wastes their energy
on boring old *ethics* nowadays, anyways?

Condoning / defending / promoting *cheating.*
Maybe it's fun — just another greasy skid down the slippery slope,
A misstep past regrettable sleaze,
beyond depressing, on its way towards
hopelessly bankrupt, across the scorched earth of
resignation to enslavement within an authoritarian Evil Empire.

Oh, right: we're already *there.* [insert sigh in square brackets]
Ah well: maybe I've got this wrong.
One can only hope, maybe, instead of cheat.

Binary Code

Welcome earthlings, puny *Homo sapiens* all, to the Digitization of the Universe.

Surely you must be feeling worn down, flattened by the extreme streaming of ones and zeroes. Binary Code! Oh yes, you were seduced by its promise: technology as saviour, the Great Progressive Hope. But you got bamboozled by the magician's misdirection, distracted by the sexy assistant. It was only ever about the monthly service fees, those corporate profits floated to off-shore accounts. Now you're bundled up in your contract for phone, cable & internet: signed, sealed & delivered, reduced to a few milliseconds of coding, flying at the speed of light through a fiber optic cable — a digital ding on your credit card. You thought TV had replaced religion as the mass opiate? Ha! Now your devices are China White, and you're a demographic algorithmic line-entry in the cells of a spreadsheet.

Oh, you've got your serialized franchise sequels of cartoon superhero tentpole popcorn blockbusters. You've got your pre-programmed hit parade, curated playlists, focus-grouped sampled mashed-up binary-coded data dumps, as you binge-watch the torrential flow of algorithmic cyber services.

And you? Yourself? Well, you're nothing but an electronic profile: an unwitting victim of the software that analyzes your preferences. You know what's been digitized? Your medical records, banking, credit cards, government files, driver's licence, health card, investment portfolio, web surfing habits: you're only ever one hack away from identity theft and fraud, because . . .

You're a bar code. A magnetic strip. A number in a data bank in a hard drive.
You're not even a bit in a byte.

You are nothing but ones and zeroes.
You are zero and nothing but one.
You are
one
zero.

Nothing.

The Non-Secrets of Life (Part One)

Work, Failure: Gravity, Balance

The first secret of life is
that there are no secrets.
Clichés, adages and maxims become so
because they are simple truth, over and over again.

Secrets, you ask?
Ok. This might be another well-known non-secret.
There is no substitute for Work Ethic.
Stop searching for shortcuts to truth.

The next un-secret could be:
Embrace Failure. Own it.
I've been told, a secret of life is the number .367 —
the lifetime batting average of Ty Cobb.
The greatest hitter of all time failed more than six times out of ten.
That should teach us something about humility
and about forgiving ourselves.

Next — might be the Law of Gravity.
What goes up, must come down.
Rivers run downhill and so will you.
And while that's happening, try to keep your balance.
Moderation.
Left, right — up, down — inside, outside —
happy, sad — through lightness and darkness,
the teeter-totter keeps pivoting
the pendulum keeps swinging.
Gravity guarantees that the orbit stays fixed
and the orbit guarantees that what goes around comes around
but the not-so-secret trick is
to keep finding your way back to the gravitational centre

and stay light on your feet, able to adjust:
roll with the punches, claim the middle ground.
The centre will never stay in one place:
it moves, just as nature itself evolves and mutates
in order to survive and progress.
But even as the evolutionary imperative
shifts the paradigm
it's no secret that
you need to try and hear your inner voice, and
adjust to your inner ear —
find the centre of balance
in the seat of your pants,
on the move,
on the fly.

The Non-Secrets of Life (Part Two)

Coming to Terms

Cathedrals are not evidence of God.
They are proof of man's imagination about God.

Nature gives us the shape of the maple leaf:
but it's human ingenuity that gives it geometry:
left and right,
north, south, east and west.

So, human — here's a thought.
Come to terms with nature
on her own terms.

Water takes the shape of the container.
You could
adapt.
Evolve.

The Non-Secrets of Life (Part Three)
Time Time Time

It's no secret —
life gets a bit easier when you
come to terms with Time.

Time is elastic.
It stretches, it shrinks.

It walks in four,
it rocks in eights,
it gets funky in sixteenths
and when it swings,
it's all good.
Saul Goodman.

Respect time. Use it.
You can't make time,
so learn to manage it.
Make the most of what
time allows.
At the same time — you must allow time
to take its own sweet time.

And now, ladies & gentlemen:

The major timeline
divides beautifully into three acts:
Past
Present and
Future.

[cont'd]

TIME

TIME

TIME

When Time Is Beautiful

The Past is beautiful
because it holds the emotions of our memories
and the narrative remains our own
privately, within ourselves
to reinterpret
to benefit our present and our future.

The Present is beautiful
because it is the only place
where the past and the future reside simultaneously.
The present is the live, vital, current location
where we bring our awareness
to the liquid stream of time.

The Future is beautiful
because it glows with potential
with the hope that springs eternal.
The future is where
infinite eternity always resides.

And now, ladies & gentlemen:

A Tragedy,
in three acts.

[cont'd]

When Time Is Ugly

The Past can be dangerous — the Land of Regret.
Can't go back and fix mistakes made:
can only visit failures hiding in your head.
A World of Sorrow & Guilt — memories of losses,
ghosts who haunt episodes of weakness,
moments when hearts were broken.
The Past can destroy ambition, productivity:
eat time, waste energy.
A Republic of Deceit
viewed through a rose-coloured rearview mirror.
Rewritten by false memory — littered with ignorance, inhumanity.
Stupid Human Tricks.

Santayana warned — don't forget, doomed to repetition:
but who wants to relive it, over and over,
becoming paralyzed — metastasized within the corruption
of echoing negativity?

It might be that some things need to be forgotten: forgiven
so that life can go on in The Present
uncluttered, unfettered, unconstrained.

But . . . **The Present** can also be a wormhole of shame
a self-perpetuating vortex of self-doubt & self-loathing.
It can be the place where The Past and The Future crowd out all hope.
Time can be ruthless: running out on you, never waiting.
You know it can, and the knowing can eat you up
here and now.

It might be Time
But — it could be us.

Plus . . . **The Future** can be the Commonwealth of Anxiety.
"What If?" What if things go wrong? Go south?
Take a turn for the worse?
We KNOW we're going to die: but what if we get sick first?
What if we lose what we've got, or screw it up?
The Future is a void of the unknown,
a dark, sinister Frontier of Stress —
the graveyard of negativity:
full of self-induced manifestations of angst,
self-fulfilling prophecies of doomsdays.

It might be The Future,
but it's probably us.

The Future in The Present

A Change in the Weather

When I am afraid
The Future is a cold hard wind
that blows straight into my face.
It seeks me out and buffets up against me,
attacking
denying
rejecting
in its furious anger.

It conspires with ancient gods
to rob me of any ambitious dreams —
scatters the words away from the poem in my head
as easily as it steals my breath and leaves me speechless,
unnerved.

It does not allow the present to arrive comfortably
in its own good time.
No — it pushes the clock hands behind me,
rushes on past
so that any road ahead
feels like the bitter ache of yesterday's mistakes
in the chill of its cruel punishment.

But when I am lighthearted, oh,
The Future gently assures
with an encouraging guiding hand
in the small of my back.
There's a natural momentum to enjoy —
the soothing spin of orbits synch and resonate —
integrated, harmonious.
Water flows downhill.

The tall grass waves,
the tree leaves dance.
It is as it should be
here in this moment.

Yet even in this calm
there is a hint of melancholy,
for it cannot last.
Nothing is forever.
I am aware of this,
even as the warm comfort rises.
I know full well
the cold will come rushing in,
eager to bully
and insist upon its agenda.

The Present Can Be a Gift

The Present can be a gift:

as Okakura Kakuzō's Taoism
teaches the art of being in the world —
this is where we're at.

"Within each human being
god meets nature and
yesterday is separated from tomorrow.
The Present is the moving infinity,
the legitimate sphere of The Relative.
Relativity seeks Adjustment.
Adjustment is Art.
The art of life lies
in a constant readjustment
to our surroundings."

The "moving infinity" of The Present
means that the "art" of the now
must also promise / contain / embody
a sense of The Future —
the universality of the infinite.

Just as
the drop is in the ocean
and the ocean's in the drop
a steady, peaceful heartbeat
holds a truth that will not stop.
To be calm, and still, and let this
moment speak to you
let the river flow on through (flow on through)

for time is like a current
and if you catch the drift

The Present

can be a gift.

ARS NOVA

2020

Do Heals Make Noise?

three-year-old frowns
at a scab on her arm

Asks her mom

"Do heals make noise?"

Txtng

Lts pla a gam
C f txtng mks us dmb r smrt.
Hw wl u knw wot I mn
f splng dznt matr?
Wot f I dnt evn bthr
wth sm vwls?

Dz it hrm
Ntlgblt
Ndrstndblt
Cmprhnsblt?

It dznt?

Fkn A!

Wt fn!

Like

similar or equal to
comparable, akin,
in some degree;
to some extent;
sort of, in a way
nearly, probably,
typical, equalling,
after the manner of;
resembling, approaching . . .

"So, like, I was riding the subway, right?
And, like, there was this guy, y'know?
And, like, he was all, like — ewww —
like, grotty, right?

So I was like, whoa, dude;
like — social distancing, y'know?
Cuz it was, like, totally uncool.

But he was, like, zoned out!
It was, like, he didn't even get it!
Y'know, like — what I was tryin' to say?!
He was, like — just — like,
starin' at me! Like, my words
were like alien or foreign or
like maybe he was just, like,
I dunno — like, trippin' or somethin' like that?

Yeah, it was, like, so frickin' weird.

So, like, anyway, that's it, really.

Like — that's all cool, right? Like,
cuz that's my BLOG for today.
So thanks for watchin', and if you, like,
think it's trill, then please hit
Like, and, like,
subscribe —
hashtag thumbsallup.
That'd be, like, *awesome.*"

The World of Song

Ev'ry song carries our sorrow
and all that sadness
fills the sky
until the clouds
release their burden
and heav'n above
begins to cry

Ev'ry song
lifts up the heartache
gets washed away
in the falling rain
then a break of dawn
conquers the horizon
so the world of song
can rise again.

The world of song
keeps the planet turning
sharing our stories
so far and wide
where the wind blows high
in the rolling thunder
in a secret whisper
in a lullaby.

Ev'ry song
is a celebration
from hallelujah
to the midnight blues
each lonely soul
grieving or rejoicing
'til a holy light
comes shinin' through.

The world of song
keeps the planet turning
sharing our stories
so far and wide
where the wind blows high
in the rolling thunder
in a secret whisper
in a lullaby.

Where the wind blows high
in the rolling thunder
in a secret whisper
in a lullaby.

Ultra-Talk!

I'm trying out a new
therapeutic coping mechanism
as a supplement to my anxiety medication —

Ultra-Talk!

Quit trying to make sense
of the random chaos:
of competing agendas for common sense
that are uncommonly self-serving.
Quit carping about
interpretations of
constitutions and declarations of
human rights that lack
equitability, plurality and neutrality.

Instead — try Ultra-Talk!

Stop worrying about global warming,
domestic terrorism, the Middle East and the Big C.
Put very little faith in science.
Lord knows you have even less faith in faith.
Abandon hope, all ye who live in fear.
Forge ahead courageously.
Buy lottery tickets instead, since
governments are more addicted
to gambling revenue anyway.
Just forget about syntax
and pay more sin tax.
Ultra-Talk!

In 1985,
long before the Twitter Prez,
Snapchat, Instagram, and
The Four Horsemen of Technology
Neil Postman opined
that we were already Amusing Ourselves to Death —

and now — yes! —
we have yet another poet (groan)
to prove it.

Ultra-Talk!

Snowflakes

Around ten quintillion water molecules
in each crystal of snow.

Water vapour
up in a cloud
condenses into droplets,
freezes into tiny bits of ice.

Water molecules bond together
forming a hexagonal crystalline lattice
with a six-fold symmetry.
Which is to say: as more water vapour condenses on its surfaces,
the ice crystals grow into hexagonal prisms.
Then as the crystals enlarge,
branches begin to form at the corners of their hexagons.

When the crystals get too heavy,
they fall through the atmosphere
towards the ground.

We call 'em snowflakes —
no two the same.

Now — some folks believe the unique nature
of every individual human being
is miraculous.
Holy.
Proof of a divine plan.

But —

just sayin' —

all the hexagonal prisms,
all the sextupled symmetry,
all the tens of quintillions of water molecules,
all the snowflakes

melt.

Dream #23,475

Sept. 16, 2018

Had a dream
a former student (generic not specific) had come back to me
with a large box.
I had helped him build the box,
to carry around all the things he would learn.
He said no one wanted him, or
the stuff in his box.
He wanted to destroy the box —
ceremoniously —
right on the exact spot where it had originally been built.

But the box couldn't
wouldn't
be broken.

I was trying to tell him
just leave it
let it go —
but he was getting angry
trying to smash the box,
and it just kept
bouncing around.

Then I woke up.

Oh Canada

started Jan. 26, 2018 in a B&B in Cincinnati, Ohio

Oh Canada
Such reluctant, guarded optimism,
modest presbyterian humility
in your sensible wardrobe —
skeptical of cocks crowing,
bully pulpits and the politics of power.

Blue by nature, red enough
for cooperative inclinations.
Apologies for intrusions.

Oh Canada
your spine of rocky granite
your heart conditioned,
seasoned through black fly summer
and pummelled by brutal winter.

Your sense is common,
your reason deliberate.
Your weathered face the product
of climate, geography and circumstance.

How vast your dominion
how true is your north
how deep lies your silent strength
to survive
to endure
to remain standing
on your guard —

Oh Canada.

GRATEFUL ACKNOWLEDGEMENTS

To the spirit of my mother, Thelma Margaret Baxter, who had the soul of an artist, struggling inside the duties and social expectations of a '50s housewife.

To advance readers, Jane Christmas and Nancy Wood.

To meaningful perspectives, sprung from the advice of Janice Carere.

To the textbook guidance from *How a Poem Moves* by Adam Sol (he showed up in one of the poems here) and *the poem is you* by Stephanie Burt, which offered both motivation and a licence to practice.

To a longtime correspondent named Scott Michael Anderson, in the fan forum on my website, who would frequently share his poems in his posts, and I thought: well, *he's* doing it — *so can I.*

To grade-school teacher Florence Herchmer.

To high school English teachers Dorothy Cameron-Monk and Margaret McLean.

To songwriters & lyricists like Bob Dylan, Paul Simon, James Taylor, Bruce Cockburn, Jimmy Webb, Johnny Mercer, Lorenz Hart and Ira Gershwin.

To the inspiration of writers like Ray Bradbury, Douglas Adams, Alice Munro, Margaret Atwood and Kurt Vonnegut Jr., and the creativity of cartoonist Gary Larson.

To musicians like Pat Metheny, Joe Pass, Larry Carlton and Steely Dan; The Beatles, Deep Purple, Yes, Led Zeppelin; Clapton, Beck, Page, Hendrix. They all contributed to the hodgepodge of my discriminating taste.

To the skillful and diplomatic editing provided to a rookie poet by Michael Holmes, Jen Albert and Shannon Parr, and the production direction from Jessica Albert and Cassie Smyth, at ECW.

To my Burlington studio soul brother, Mike Shotton.

And finally: to readers like you, Your Honour.

PHOTO BY STUART HENDRIE

Rik Emmett is in four "Halls" and two "Walks of Fame." After 12 platinum LPs in his Triumph years, Rik produced 20 indie projects, from rock and blues to jazz, folk and classical. His latest release is *Folk Songs for the Farewell Bonfire*. An avowed family man, he's been married for 45 years; he was also a *Guitar Player* magazine columnist for more than a dozen years and an educator for a few decades at Humber College. Rik is Artistic Director Emeritus of the Song-Studio Workshop, and a published poet and cartoonist. He lives in Burlington, Ontario.